AF264418

Private Lives, God's Eyes, and the Pregnant Now

27 poems by 9 poets

Edited by
Marilyn Wolf

ISBN: 978-0-9989160-4-0 (Paperback)

Library of Congress Control Number: 2026909816

Cover design: Aleksander Blowkowsky

Printed by Marilyn Wolf, LLC, in the United States of America.

Marilyn Wolf, LLC
8594 E 116th St
Apt 419
Fishers, IN 46038

www.wolfen25.net

Introduction

Private Lives, God's Eyes, and the Pregnant Now: 27 Poems by 9 Poets has three sections on specific poetic techniques with three poems by three poets. Three sections, nine poets, 27 poems. Though cohesion is important, as an editor, I want writers to have freedom of interpretation. I gave the poets only general guidelines on each technique. This may be first in a series of similar books; it is yet to be determined.

I'm in a Master of Fine Arts (MFA) program at Butler University in Indianapolis. When I proposed the idea of this book series to my classmates, Jenny Walton and Paige Wyatt, we thought it sounded like fun. We also thought it would be fun to have Walton-Wolf-Wyatt as authors.

We were discussing different anthropomorphic forms in class; I used that as the basis for the first section. **Anthropomorphism** is the assignment of human qualities to non-human things. Poets in this section are Jenny Walton, Marilyn Wolf, and Paige Wyatt.

When Section One was done, I extended the project and made two more. I chose the techniques in the last two sections because the invited poets tended to use them in their work.

The second section uses assonance or consonance in poetry. **Assonance** is the repetition of vowel sounds; sometimes called vowel rhyme. **Consonance**, as used in these poems, refers to shared consonants; sometimes in proximity; sometimes throughout the poem. Poets in this section are Tony Brewer, Hiromi Yoshida, and Chris Dean.

Poetry in the third section uses words, phrases, or metaphors that **evoke sensory responses**: taste, sight, touch, hearing, smell. The poets in this section are Curtis Crisler, Ron Whitehead, and Thomas Kneeland.

We hope you enjoy it.
Marilyn Wolf, Editor

Table of Contents

Section 3, Senses

On the eve of my twenty-year high school reunion
by Jenny Walton

The person that I thought I would probably be someday is the
one hanging around just out of the shot
 on this day

offering unsolicited second opinions about a few of my
choices.

If I close my eyes, I can smell her shampoo because / the
person that I thought I would probably be someday,

                    she showers every morning.

She drops in / a delinquent producer bored and a little
embarrassed by this low-budget project I'm directing—this
make-it-up-as-we-go thing
  that keeps on

        going

and going and going and going and / going and going and
going and going and going and going and going and

going and—if you ask her

simply not
                                amounting
all the going matched by a growing shit list for me
        provided by the person that I thought I would
        probably be someday

a list of everything I can't do yet
          can't claim, can't buy, can't figure, can't wrangle,
can't say, can't own, can't own up to.

I am simply not
amounting on schedule.

How is this what thirty-nine looks like? Haunted by teen
dreams of neuroanatomy and law school, of being like
actually really wealthy, obnoxiously well dressed, healthy on
purpose.

 Is this the crisis?   /   The midlife thing?

Haunted I drive a fifteen year old Subaru Forester with no
A/C in ninety degree heat to another hourly job,
                                        while
                        the person that I thought
I would probably be someday bitches at me / relentlessly
from the backseat about what I could've been if I hadn't—

I slam the brakes. *What?*

If I hadn't what?

Being Late goes to therapy
by Jenny Walton

Welcome, Mx. Late. It's lovely to see you. Please make yourself comfortable. And as you do, I'll remind you that our appointment will end on the hour even though we're off to, well, what I mean to say is . . .

> What you mean to say is that we're off to a late start. I'm familiar.

Yes, well, no harm. We'll make the most of the Time we have. Why don't you begin by sharing what prompted your decision to come here today?

> Yeah, okay, so people don't get me, you know? They're all like *life is about living in the present* and shit. But the second I show my face, they're yelling at their kids about socks or driving like a maniac through residential neighborhoods even though those streets are crawling with cats. And, I mean, it's really, like really starting to fuck with me.
>
> Oh, man, is it okay if I say that? If I say *fuck*?

You're encouraged to use whatever language helps you best express yourself.

Cool, cool. Okay, so I guess that's my issue. In a nutshell. People seem to think I'm a problem. I mean, god forbid I go to some job interview or a wedding. They go ballistic. Like total toddler-meltdown apeshit, you know? Like Time was their special toy, and I took it—and I mean that, people act like Time is their fucking toy.

Interesting that you mention Time. How would you describe your relationship?

Look, Time can be a smug piece of shit, don't get me wrong. But you can't believe everything you hear about him. Honestly, he's not all that bad.

Oh. I guess I didn't realize Time had a gender.

Really? I mean, it seems pretty obvious to me.

A man's treasures
> *after Charles Simic*
> by Jenny Walton

Small Loss stops by the city dump on his way home from
work. And over the fence he tosses his load of loose hairs,
> receipts,
>> pen caps,
> stale bits of oat cereal,
>> and today
> an unsettling number of pennies.

> He's exhausted

and filthy from crawling under unmade beds and behind
refrigerators. From digging through backpacks and beneath
car seats.   He thinks

> *people used to be cleaner*
> as he pushes through his own front door in the
> dark.

He hangs his keys / on the key hook / places his shoes on
the shoe rack / his jacket in the coat closet /

Calls down the stark white hall to his wife / who at this
moment is making a sort of kitchen sink soup. A thing
she does from time to time

because she's embarrassed
whenever he picks up a stray clove of garlic or finds a potato

gone to rot in the root cellar.
A hazard of the trade,
he shrugs when it happens.

But tonight / no chit chat / no meandering through the
working memory of the day / tonight,

Small Loss, lost in his thoughts, reaches into the deep wells
of his worn pockets,

pockets that now hold the minutes and hours unaccounted
for / salvaged from the dump /

he methodically organizes them by size and weight
along the long / open counter

where they glow warm like a salt lamp

where they smell like butter and honey

Ménage à Thought
by Marilyn Wolf

Part One

"Tell me a story," he said.
"Once upon a time," she began,
"there was a princess."
No, wrong story.
No princesses here.
"It was a dark and stormy night,"
well, yes it was, but that's not the story either.

She walked the street to ease her mind.
wind whipped her scarf, thoughts
the way he had whipped her skin
with a newspaper, of all things.
Just enough to take her thoughts, make them his.
He controlled her thoughts as she had never known.
She wanted more.

She felt her thoughts start to follow her
Closely then farther behind then skipping beside.
They hadn't done that before.
She had seen them but not as lively as this.
For a second they preceded her.
Turned the corner before she did.
"Interesting," she thought.
She followed them.

They had seen other thoughts
and skipped to join them.
She and another woman watched them.

7

"Are these other thoughts hers?" she wondered.
All the thoughts swirled, gathered, changed colors
But muted, almost pastel.
Not the colors she expected from their energy.

Her thoughts sorted themselves into striated patterns,
newsprint but with colors.
"Interesting," she thought.
She followed them.
They were the words he and she had said
moving to the rhythm of his arm
as the newsprint came down onto her skin.
The other thoughts watched hers and followed.
She and the other woman followed, too.

All the thoughts walked, flowed, skipped
to his door. Both women looked at each other.
The thoughts became smoke and flew away.
She opened the door.
Both women walked in.

"Interesting," she thought.
She wanted more.

Part Two

She followed the other woman.
Watched her hips roll
Side to side, up and down.
Her calves tensed and lifted those hips
As she climbed the stairs.
"Interesting," she thought.
She wanted more.

The man was painting a canvas.
His thoughts were drawing on the walls.
The thoughts the women had left outside
Were at the windows wanting in.
No order, no pattern, many colors.
Thoughts from both women
Intertwined, interconnected,
Just as they would soon be.

His thoughts stopped drawing and watched them.
He continued painting,
Knowing they were there,
ignored them both.
His thoughts surrounded them
Called them to the window.
The women let their thoughts inside.
They moved toward the floor
His hovered directly above.
"Interesting," she thought.

Her thoughts reached toward her.
His thoughts struck the tendril.
It recoiled. His thoughts swirled,
Danced, celebrated the control.

Then struck the women's thoughts
From all sides, lightly but directly.
Female thoughts danced, shivered, vibrated.
They wanted more.

Female thoughts began forming
Newsprint patterns in vibrant colors.
He understood and stopped painting.
The women watched him
Stride toward them, breathing deeply.
They held hands.

He picked up the newspaper.
His painting was a ménage à trois
The three of them
Intertwined, interconnected.
"Interesting," she thought.
She wanted more.

Part Three

Wind from the open window
blew his thoughts
to the corner of the room.
Hers still cowered and writhed on the floor.

Female thought tendrils
reached to surround
and anchor the women's ankles
holding them for him.
They hadn't done that before.
He came closer
his thoughts clustered and swirled
behind him
silent
watching
wanting   to participate
knowing he wouldn't allow it yet.

"Interesting," she thought.
She wanted more.

They could feel his breath
even from where he was standing.
He's electric.
His thoughts charge him
and he they.

The other woman's hand
flutters against her's
feels her heat
hears her breath break.

The painting melts to the floor.
The women watch the colors
move toward his feet
colors entangle his thoughts
pulling them down.
Thoughts painting
move up his ankles
forming letters at his knees.

Female thoughts tentatively
reach toward his thoughts
Such beautiful colors
thoughts entwine.

All thoughts and painting
splash to the floor around his feet.
Female thoughts
male thoughts
painting
form into
vibrant
silent
words
between him and the women.

It's they who form the
ménage à trois
as the people watch.

Letters
thoughts
paint
words

in out
screaming
grunting
silently.
He and the women
watch.
With a sickening shudder
it's over.

The other woman faints.
The man stares at the thoughts,
still holding the newspaper.
She turns and walks
downstairs
outside.
"Interesting," she thought.
No more.
No more.

Previously published in *Scuzzbucket*.

God's Eyes
by Paige Wyatt

God said that a dunk
in the church bathtub
would save Momma and Daddy
from disappearing
down
plastic orange pain pill bottles.

God heard twelve year old me
cry as I sewed holes in my clothes
cooked pancakes on a gasless stove
while my parents got high.

God watched me
beat my way through mosh pits
get kicked out of the church band
pick fights for fun
break
a drug dealer's jaw.

God gave me
a son at twenty-one.
I put down my drumsticks
and picked up a baby bottle.

God showed me how
to be had and held, until
the groom decided
he was done. So

God was silent when I kissed
her
and for the first time in years,
I sighed.

God quit watching.

Recipe for an Ex

by Paige Wyatt

I slice off my double chin
with a carver's knife,
run the fat beneath water,
watch the blood trickle
into the disposal,
pat it dry with a paper towel,
glue it to his girlfriend's face
so every time he kisses her,
he looks at me.

I scrape away my chest tattoo,
with a cheese cleaver
rend it to fine black flakes,
and pour them into his pepper shaker
when he seasons the potatoes she makes,
he will consume my flesh.

I plunge a melon baller
into his navy blue eyes
they bounce onto the white carpet
in his new home.
Using the little red stapler,
attach them to his anus
so he can see his shit
as clearly as I can.

Anxiety Machine
by Paige Wyatt

Dusk cloaked, spindly branches
        dressed in purple blooms reach
    their claws into my chest and pull.

                    Their venom sizzles in my blood,
        rushes through too narrow veins popping,
    blistering delicate walls.

                    Life froths.

As much as I hate this, it suits me,
        though seeking its soothing makes me too much.
                    I hunger for words and hands and light
        and

                    their devouring.

I beg you to see the way words impact
        the perception of my unlovable body–
                    how music transforms disgust into desire.

                    I would go back to golden biscuits
        browning,
            Dove soap soaked in warm sink water,
    bleary-eyed and naming new wrinkled skin

                    if I could.

But it's beneath the sizzling that hurts most.
 Breaking innocence with purple links in
 white search boxes:
      "Narcotics addiction symptoms."

  Does this live in my bloodstream?

Belly of the Beast
by Tony Brewer

Take care in there
where we keep elites

code for bros
that bloviate the echo
their fathers' fathers made
in boardrooms the world
overlorded

overloaded with shame
below their pay grade

forgetting everyone
is biodegradable
and rich as much as poor
are digestible

Fear of Replacement
by Tony Brewer

All the dead are still living
asking for a blanket
so here's forgiveness
You're welcome
silence and beyond

Wait long enough
death becomes a stage
unlit and crowdless

They can make more of you
when you cannot object
so sayeth the writing
on the wall
refusing gravity as truth does
when dreaming feels like logic death

Notice how toward ends
it's all breathing and breath
and making amends
in the movie in my head

Some kind of record
of some kind of truth
like documentaries teach histories
without actually being true

Filled with tons of facts
nearly entirely you
but just a body
beginning to end

Private Lives We Share
By Tony Brewer

All artists arrive at awakenings
afraid alter-egos are accidents

The intelligentsia of agony
with its right way of show
attached to wrong ways of tell

knows ghosts create
inside spooky sweaty garrets
artists inhabit with dead artists

picking up loose ideas
knocking knickknacks off shelves
like a geist or
naughty necessary cats

I know my art history
and still wind up the asshole
in scenarios structured on paper
but IRL turn out to be rough drafts

dutiful in the doodling
but life takes far too much
free labor to get it right
at least at first

**Response to Renée Nicole Macklin's
"On Learning to Dissect Fetal Pigs"**
by Hiromi Yoshida

sepia reek of fetal pig feet—
rowdy media vultures drown,
formaldehyde slick; normalize
askew gunshots—trigger the fringe;
finger exhibits (whose asymmetric
labels hang
loose)—smear dogeared
biology textbooks—
(dissection is dissent); existential
crises cry peekaboo; pluck
out the sun's sullen
eyeball gingerly
with pincers (sticky and
epithelial); peel off the
gelled target's cello-
phane eyelid—
these assonant
days of dissonance.

Icarus Stigmata
by Hiromi Yoshida

Icarus blinks, feeling
the stigmata of the blazing
sun upon his pale
shoulders, the weight of
the osier framework
chafing his straining back.
His seaward gaze
drops into the green
void—his destiny
swirling there—past the choppy
mirror surface; the
opaque bird rises—
and Icarus contemplates a
sunward flight.

Super Bowl LX Halftime Show
By Hiromi Yoshida

Bad Bunny in the sun
bringing in the bling and a
fistful of dollars
into the immaculate space of
clumsy exchange between
fumbling quarterback
hands; makeshift sugar cane
plantations sprout around
electricity poles—the casita
overflows tricks, and the Americas
become one borderless continent
of acrobatic signifiers
and icons slipping past translators
of Spanish into English and
ICE agents spraying bullets into
windshields (bad
onomatopoeia); always
blinking, concocting incantations,
beneath floodlights—graffiti of
words released—
emancipation of the
grey-eyed dove; Bad Bunny
peels an orange like the eyelid
of the sun.

insomnia
by Chris Dean

I was 11 when I learned
that death
wasn't always a release,
that the truth didn't always
set you free
and that tears of relief and grief
could look the same
to those who'd spent a lifetime
pretending not to see.

I was 21 when I learned
about the anger
that could live in a fractured soul,
that time and distance weren't enough
to keep the skeletons in their closet
and that sleep could be a grave robber
digging up bodies of the past
Night after night
for your own private autopsy theater.

I was 31 when I learned
not all knights
rode in on white steeds
to slay dragons and save the maiden fair.
That the real hero was the one
willing to walk with you during the Witching Hour
and hold your hand while you screamed your demons
back to their hell
giving you the strength to rescue yourself.

I was 41 when I learned
you could mourn for the living
because the dead didn't always die
and soulless didn't always mean corpse.

Sometimes they still called twice a year
to haunt your Birthdays and Christmases
like some kind of cheap Dickens knock-off
and the pain of the loss was real
whether you answered the phone or not.

I was 51 when I learned
nightmares could walk
in the daylight of photo albums,
random Netflix movies or family gatherings.
That phrases like, "I've worked through it,"
and, "What doesn't kill me makes me stronger, right?"
were just empty words to avoid opening mental mausoleums
because sometimes the dark you're most afraid of
lives on in your memories.

Before I'm 61
I want to learn
to be my own Van Helsing
and drive stakes through the hearts
of the creatures that have haunted my entire life.
To write light that burns away
the shadows of my youth and steals their ability
to Boogeyman my sleep and waking hours
so I can live without fear.

And even though I know
some scars are so old and so deep
that new growth will never fade
the angry red to rose-petal pink,
I still have hope
that one day
the dead will finally rest
in whatever peace they can find
so that I can too.

Previously published in "we're all stories in the end" from
Storeyline Press.

the pregnant now of today
by Chris Dean

I came out of the dark
where I wander from time to time
to taste the light as it falls on my skin
lick it from my lips and arms
feel its warmth on my tongue
as it slides to my belly
lighting fires of passion
where it lands in the pit

I came out of the dark
to eat the wind
snap at dragonflies and chase inspiration
a puppy at its heels
playing fetch with ideas and words
all boundless energy
to mark the world as mine

I came out of the dark
to walk proudly through the day
tits low head high
to show the young age is not the enemy
to hold its hand down the sidewalk
two lovers in sync
to kiss its mouth and swallow its feel
as we laugh in discomfort's face

I came out of the dark
to place truth on the table
a dish whose flavor only comes when shared
served on rusty plates
gold forks paper cups
always paired with a glass of gratitude
the bottle passed freely between winos in the park

I came out of the dark
leaving bread crumbs behind
for friends to find
strangers to follow
for the birds of need to feed on the stale crumbs
while singing holy holy holy
this is life exactly as it's meant to be

I came out of the dark
done with rest
shaking the droplets of cold from my fur
and flicking bits of loneliness from my teeth
ready to wrap myself in the desires of the moment
while I go naked underneath
squatting to touch the earth
steady eyes empty from the night
hungry to be filled with the pregnant now of today

Previously published *BeatLife Magazine* and as "pyre" in *Keeping the Flame Alive Press*.

my body
by Chris Dean

My body, my mind,
my thick-ass thighs.
This space…
this safe space,
this sacred space,
where I am my own
ear of God
without need for
intercession of
priestess or priest.

Where I offer
myself contrition.
Where I grant
myself redemption.
Where every night,
I crawl into bed
with a heart and soul
that's clean.

Where I sleep soundly
on my pillow,
swim warmly
in my dreams
and roll thunderously
in the arms
that wrap me in their calm
after the sweat cools
from the fury
of our storm.

Previously published in *Tickets to Midnight Vol III* from
Pure Sleeze Press.

it got cold today
by Curtis Crisler

the winds blew them damn black oaks
east—bending them like elbows, like knees,
like blades of grass after feet press them blades
towards earth. *probably, god, just jogging.*

Coming Back to Deep Dirt
—for Stephon
By Curtis Crisler

Talking to your bones
under six feet of rich
Louisiana red clay and
dirt, I can never hear you-
r come backs. All you
ever bellow gets muffled
in rich earth, tight roots,
before it reaches the surfac-
e. Your mouth full with
soil, grubs, and worms.
You always talked with
your head down, to where
I have to ask, "What did
you say?" You'd say,
"Huh?" I still look for answer-
s every time I come to
get my fill of fried oysters
and beignets. It's been
seven whole years sinc-
e my last visit. There are
more weeds, instead of
baby's breath and patience
roaming around you and
your headstone brothe-
r. It's on me—it's gotten
easy to be lonely amongst
those who love you.
There are no lips keeping
me away from you,
not really. I've neve-
r missed a hug so much,

until your arms made
an X across your bod-
y, within an embroidered
lace-stitched casket,
and life said no more.

Shuffling Paper
by Curtis Crisler

In grad school, you fall
in love with everybody…
the professor who clicks
similes between her lips,
like putting cartridges
into a .9mm clip. The student
who shows her whale tail,
and has you dreaming
about them dry jail cells.
Maintenance, who wears
those tight ass Dickies
and makes you want to
enter the hell of the supply
room. Don't do it. Don't
have the academic cops
chase you down through
your cv. But, I knew a girl.
No, a woman. She was
full of nitroglycerin and worry.
So much so that attendance
in her class was the best
in the department due to
her saying, "I have cancer
and I'm here everyday.
What's your excuse." Once
she lost a vial of medicine
and bout went crazy
thinking she'd killed some-
one, due to her life. But,
it was found. Due to
her life, another young
man feel in love with her.
Her bandana. Her sad
eyes. Her tiredness. Who
does that? And love was

found. And they got married.
And I could have them in
a poem about configurating
their way through the
toughest part of individuality.
Of absence. Of words and
their meaning. Sometimes
all the papers with words
say nothing but I'm in the
middle of it all. Right now.

Comes Night And Wind
By Ron Whitehead

   1
I dream for the desert, the Indian land:
To live in a hut, drift to sleep
warmed by the fading wolf song.
I make six-foot womanly vases
and paint them naked with bird and animal heads.
Times at night
I put down the clay
and play my violin, accompany the wolf.
Comes wind,
weaves the night, violin, wolf song.
Comes wind,
weaves the night, violin, wolf song.

   2
Trees bud and bloom.
The evening star appears.
I sit by the still waters.
the moon like a shadow,
bright gold dipped in pale silver,
rests gently upon the waters.
The trees bend to listen
as I sing to Otsego
and Susquehanna: cool, calm, clear.
The notes vibrate the night, they touch
the moon like a shadow,
bright gold dipped in pale silver.

   3
Through a raven's eyes,
from high above,
the old truck is seen
winding southward through
the hunting grounds of Kentucky.

Her soft lips kiss the colored stars,
the red giants, the blue dwarfs,
on my chest. Her tongue
draws
a slow line round
the blue, green and yellow lotus flowered
sun at the center of my pyramid
and as I breathe her fiery wild red hair
her lips wash my orange lightning
bolts, wash them clean of color and sweat.
My love,
these bodies, our home
in this windless place,
prevail for pulsing moments but
your touch,
your lips, your kiss
last forever and through a raven's eyes,
from high above,
an invisible force, a sacred wind sings:
Our wind hewn love
shall be our palace.

Mosaic
By Ron Whitehead

Many people attended your annual Mary Magdalene
Black Madonna party.
The backyard bonfire burned bright.
I was drinking too much. I was filled with a rage
that had been building for years.
I was trying to figure out who in hell you really were.
I stumbled and tripped into then over the bonfire.
My pants caught fire.
I brushed the fire off and walked on.
You caught up with me at the end of the street, near the river.
You offered to give me a ride back to my writing hermitage,
miles away.
I called you every name in the book and walked on, into the
night,
finally making it back to my studio
on Cherokee Road in The Highlands.
The first two years of our relationship, of our love,
    was a raging fire.
Then you said, "No more. I'm done."
I was at death's door. My liver was shot,
    from drinking too much.
I was told that if I didn't stop
I wouldn't live past the end of the year.
And I had never met anyone who evoked so many emotions.
I swore I would never fall in love again. But I had fallen.
I was madly in love with Jinn.
So I stopped drinking. Jinn gave me another chance.
In a year my liver was healed.
On Summer Solstice Jinn and I will celebrate
    fifteen years of love.
Our love is a mosaic made of thousands of
    multi-colored stories,
from swimming naked in the Blue River,
    with snow on the banks,

to tripping through the Black Madonna bonfire, to climbing
The Viking Mountain in Iceland, to wandering the streets
of Tallinn and Tartu in Estonia, to transporting hundreds
of lost dogs to new homes, Jinn Bug and I walk together,
hand in hand, in love.

The Greatest Wisdom is Love
by Ron Whitehead

Define wisdom. Define love.
Which is greater, wisdom or love?
Would I rather have good judgment
or be in love?
At 75 years of age I say,
Throw good judgment out the damn window.
And to hell with definitions.
There is no good definition,
no rational explanation for love.
Call love irrational behavior, madness. insanity.
I have never experienced a more exalted state
in my entire life than being in love.
Without love life is a broken dream.
Give me love or give me death.
Without love I cannot rest.
There is no life without love.
The greatest wisdom is love.

overnight lows
by Thomas Kneeland

However, no one knows the day or the hour when
these things will happen, not even the angels in heaven
or the Son himself. Only the Father knows.
— Matthew 24:36

We knew what we were walking into on that rainy,
    overcast day, hands clenching
the sides of voting machines like last lovers' closure
    — a divorce for the times,
because there's no more fire to fuel the bones of mothers
    who weep silently
on loveseats after putting babies to sleep.

First cloud after the storm breaks. Two breaths of warm wind
    roll back
billows to show a hazy, blue sky. Trees crack & break
    from lightning bolts
the size of pencils, their width scribbled along remains
    of tree stumps.
May as well be gravestones now. A young man scrapes
    his last name in the skin of dying bark.

Fire erupts from a nearby bush. Seven vultures hover above
like a baby's mobile, waiting for the moment one of us
    decides
to stop breathing. How do you stop the bleeding,
when all you know is to be bled dry?

walk with me
by Thomas Kneeland

"The stars will talk to us
if we just have enough sense to listen."
— Nikki Giovanni

If you ever wake up & not find me next to you,
join me downstairs at the kitchen island
where we made our first memory of this home.

Find me hunched over, writing to the warm fire
of a salt lamp, waiting for your hands to tell me
everything will be ok. After a while,

my body will curve into yours, eyes aglaze in disbelief
that after all this time, you were the one He had for me.
& I'll hold you in my warm spaces, just like this—

remind you of the night I listened to the stars:
how they told me to hear you so that I could see you.
& now, I listen: your voice, a crackling fire.

I crawl & nestle beside it, return to the dreamscape
I find myself in most nights, near the water where
we watched the stars watch us fall for the first time.

promised land
after Nikki Giovanni
by Thomas Kneeland

Wind be nimble, gust be quick, spirit light flame on this here
    candle wick,
for life be rushin from ev'ry which way, then death come
    crawlin to snatch it away.

Baby girl wakes up with bright eyes, from dreamin of
    sugar plum pies.
Made her dough from scratch, sifted flour & sugar butta &
    watched it rise.

watched it rise watched it rise
watched it rise watched it rise

Cooled it down in the freezer, cut us both a slice.
    Ain't nothin wrong with a slice,
ain't nothin wrong with two or three,
    long as we both get our fair share —

I do right by you & you by me.

But fools wake up in the arena, eyes salt-crusted &
    glossed over with greed
salivating at the lineup of sweet treats, reaching for dough
    their hands didn't knead.

& don't you think it's time we collect the spoons, the forks,
    the knives we hammered
over hot coals while they spat in our faces,
    waitin to be fed our manna?

There's just enough for us to eat now, after so long we toil,
wand'rin round in your wilderness waitin for your
    spoils to spoil.

Biographies
In alphabetical order by last name.

Tony Brewer is a poet and audio artist from Bloomington, Indiana. He has published 13 books and chapbooks, most recently *Water Witch* (Pure Sleeze Press). Tony has been offering Poetry On Demand at coffeehouses, museums, cemeteries, churches, bars, and art and music festivals for over 15 years and was named Indiana's 2024 Literary Champion by the Eugene and Marilyn Glick Indiana Authors Awards.

Curtis Crisler has written 13 books, with more always in process. He has received multiple awards and grants and is the Indiana Poet Laureate; his term has been extended to four years. His work exhibits what he calls an urban Midwestern sensibility (uMs) — "the community and creativity of the varied relationships of descendants from the first through second waves of the southern migration, exploring their connections to place/environment, history, family, and self." He also created the poetry form the *sonastic* and the Indiana Chitlin Circuit. Crisler is Professor of English at Purdue University Fort Wayne. http://poetcrisler.com/#home

Chris Dean, Indiana Beat Poet Laureate (2025-2027) is a storyteller, graphic designer, and Magpie Poet who writes from the heart of Indiana where they live with their husband and too many cats to mention. They are the co-founder and managing editor of Keeping the Flame Alive Press and author of three full length books of poetry, *tales from a broken girl, we're all stories in the end*, and *pyre*.

Thomas Kneeland is the Pushcart-nominated author of the chapbook, *We Be Walkin' Blackly in the Deep*. His writing explores ancestry, ecological memory, and the effects of intergenerational trauma in Black, Afro-Latine, and Afro-Indigenous family dynamics. A recent recipient of the Edward Stanley Award for poems published in Prairie Schooner, his publication credits include *Obsidian: Literature & Arts in the African Diaspora, Southern Humanities Review, Hayden's Ferry Review, The Rumpus*, and elsewhere. Kneeland was recently nominated for *Hayden's Ferry Review's* Best of Small Fiction Anthology. Named a 2025 Emerging Scholar by *The EDU Ledger*, Kneeland is currently an Assistant Professor of English at Anderson University.

Jenny Walton is a lifelong Hoosier, a practicing poet, an INFP, an Enneagram Five with a Four wing, a Taurus sun, a Pisces moon, and a Capricorn rising. She likes to ask people questions and to sit outside by herself. She is member number 65,208 of the Cloud Appreciation Society and is employed by the Indianapolis Public Library. Recently, she learned—and would like for you to know—that most people breathe incorrectly. You might want to look into it when you get a minute. Her favorite foods in order and with butter are potatoes, corn, and pasta. She is currently the Co-Editor of *Booth*.

Ron Whitehead Poet, writer, editor, publisher, professor, scholar, activist, U.S. National Lifetime Beat Poet Laureate Whitehead, who grew up on a farm in Kentucky, is the author of over 40 books and over 40 albums. Alan Ginsberg characterized him as an "energetic Bodhisattvic poetic spirit," and Lawrence Heringhetti as "sowing the dragon's teeth of a new heroics." *OUTLAW POET: The Legend of Ron Whitehead*, a feature-length documentary (Storm Generation Films/Dark

Star TV) is now available for streaming via Amazon Prime Films Documentaries.

Marilyn Wolf lives in Indiana and writes poetry, prose, and essays. She is published in anthologies, Indiana's Poetry Archive, displayed in online and physical galleries, and more. She has two books of poetry, *In Celebration of the Death of Faeries* and *The Guy: Private Edition*. She is a past 1st VP, Poetry Society of Indiana, and current Director, Indiana Writers Center. https://wolfen25.net/

Paige Wyatt (she/her) is a Midwestern lesbian writer and magazine editor. She serves as the co-managing editor for *Dogwood Alchemy Art and Literary Magazine* and is a proud member of STFU Art Collective. Her work has been published with *Genrepunk Magazine, Beyond the Veil Press', We Do Not Need Permission To Rise: LGBTQ+ Poetry & Art Anthology*, and others. She doesn't spend as much time talking to the dead these days, but she travels full time around the USA with her family and eats too much mac 'n' cheese. You can find her posting memes on Instagram @paigeotto__

Hiromi Yoshida is the author of two full-length poetry collections: *Green Roses Bloom for Icarus*, and *Icarus Redux*; and six poetry chapbooks: *Icarus in Crete, Umami, Icarus Superstar, Icarus Hieroglyph, Epicanthus*, and *Icarus Burning*. She is a finalist for the New Women's Voices Poetry Prize sponsored by Finishing Line Press, and a semifinalist for the Gerald Cable Book Award sponsored by Silverfish Review Press. She is also the editor of *Stormwash: Environmental Poems* (vol. 1 & 2); poetry editor of *Flying Island Journal*; and chair of the Writers Guild at Bloomington. She curates the

Guild's Last Sunday Poetry reading series and teaches poetry for the Indiana Writers Center.